Psychological Power

Power to Control Minds

Rick Markley

Table of Contents

Introduction

It is possible to come up with any number of reasons why taking control of minds should be viewed as important. Oftentimes, it depends upon the situation.

For instance, let's say you're someone who tends to feel overpowered by a talking dynamo of the opposite sex. You know, you tend to just throw in several "uh-huhs" where you feel they're appropriate because that's about all the fast-talking other party is allowing you to do! Don't be intimidated or allow yourself to be railroaded into listening (not conversing) to something you're not even remotely interested in.

If you're worried about being perceived as rude by not listening to them go on and on about something that's not the least bit intriguing to you, consider this - it's actually more rude to pretend to care about that topic, and mislead them into thinking you might like to go to the next miniature dollhouse convention that comes to town! (Or whatever they've been yapping about).

Now, that's not to say that you shouldn't care what the other person has to say - not at all. But if you really have no input other than "uh-huh" now and again, it's not really a conversation, is it? Letting it drag on and on adds nauseam and really serves no purpose, other than to drain your energy and waste your time. Taking control of this type of pseudo-conversation and turning it into a real one is a valuable skill, and well worth cultivating.

In a scenario like the one just described, you can actually get a word in edgewise by interjecting a question, and then gradually maneuvering the conversation in the direction you'd prefer. In other words, to convert this to an actual two-way communication, you might (at a key point) say, "Oh, wow!

I remember feeling that way once, and there's a movie that I really love that made that point so well. Have you ever seen Hereafter?" If the response is "no," you have the perfect opportunity to explain the plot briefly, and switch the subject to one that you actually will enjoy. Or even to get the other person talking about movies in general, if that's something that you find more interesting than their first topic.

Or choose a book, or piece of music that you really love, so you are shifting gears towards something that you are comfortable, confident and interested. If the other person is someone you'd really like to get to know better, this is also a great way to discover some common ground, for future conversations.

So being in control of a mind, even for a brief period in the grand scheme of things, can help you diffuse tension - often for the other party, as well as yourself. It can also help you come across as more confident, outgoing and as someone who's interested in many things, and in other people.

1: How to be in Control when you are talking to Someone

In this section we'll look at a few ways to take control when you're talking to someone. Some of these ideas are simple so we can cover those in a few lines while some require a more detailed explanation and an example. Still, don't overlook the power of a principle just because it is simple. When you stack all the simple ideas, it can dramatically improve your ability to take charge.

Whether you're talking with a family member, significant other/spouse, there are many advantages to perfecting the art of redirecting, or taking control of a conversation.

Know your goal for the conversation

Whenever possible, prior to having the conversation, make sure that the right people will be included. Keep the meeting open only to those who fit into this category, as others might create distraction.

Granted, many conversations start spontaneously, and you may not have a firm objective or outcome in mind at the beginning. But it's still possible to take control. Here's an example:

As soon as you get home from work, your "S.O." starts the conversation with, "Honey, I really want to go out for Chinese food tonight. I'm really craving for some Egg Fu Young."

You just had Chinese food for lunch so you're not exactly too crazy about this idea. Still, you like to compromise and keep everyone happy, so you make the following suggestion; "Yes, Uncle Ming's has great food. So good in fact, I ate lunch there today with my boss."

Now, I'm willing to go there again for dinner if you're really craving for Chinese food. But what do you think about this? Let's jump online real quickly and read some reviews of that new Thai/Mexican/Italian (your choice) restaurant that you've been wanting to try out - you know, the one that recently opened nearby? If that sounds like something different and interesting, we could give that a try. What do you think?"

This way you have offered to go somewhere you know your S.O. has wanted to check out, but have also successfully extricated yourself from having an overdose of Uncle Ming! Simply by suggesting an alternative, you took control of the conversation.

Assume a powerful physical presence

This is particularly effective if you're meeting with someone who wants something from you. Sitting on a chair that's slightly higher than the one they'll be sitting on is an old "trick of kings." You're not going to be on a throne, of course, but just a slight height advantage (3 or 4 inches taller) can make a big impression.

It's also a good way to redirect focus to stand up as a way of indicating the conversation is concluded, or to get up and move a few steps, as though you're deep in thought (and you may well be, strategizing your next point!)

When you're on your "home turf" and really want to terminate the conversation, for example, just do the following, smiling politely the entire time:

Stand up, smile sincerely, go across the door and open it, maintaining eye contact and continuing to smile, genuinely. Say something to the effect of, "This has been great. Thank you so much for coming here to meet me! I know you have a busy schedule. I have another appointment in just a few minutes, but we'll be in touch. I appreciate your time..." (Whatever best suits the occasion).

Standing up generally takes the other party by surprise, especially if they're still talking! But it's a nonverbal way of getting your point across without having to come up with words, which may not have done the trick!

Use an authoritative but pleasant voice

Speak from a place of power and calm. This doesn't mean to lull them into a state of submission! Exude enthusiasm while coming across as the expert on - well, the things in which you are an expert.

Smiling frequently while discoursing and using humor when it fits easily keeps others at ease and more likely to follow what you're saying, rather than leaning toward "lecturing," which tends to promote loss of interest quickly.

Eliminate all distractions

When you choose the meeting point, you are more in control of the environment of the conversation. So whenever possible, grab the opportunity to choose the venue, particularly for a very important conversations using a little aforethought, not only for your own point-making ability, but also to show the other party you care enough to pick a quiet place where you can hear them clearly as well.

Ask questions to engage interaction

Ask questions and establish yourself as the "alpha" person. When you're asking questions, you're creating rapport, an interactive exchange, rather than pushing for a "filibuster."

Remember, if you keep the conversation more casual and friendly than formal and dictatorial, you'll be more successful in keeping control. It reminds me of a very old saying, "You catch more flies with honey than with vinegar."

The power of surrender

Sometimes there is tremendous amount of power that can be achieved by the simple act of surrender. What I mean by this is relaxing and detaching from any attachment to the outcome of the conversation.

Now this does not mean that you are completely giving up on your objective - far from it! But when you remain flexible as to how you go about attaining your desired outcome, in other words, when you "go with the flow," oftentimes you can more readily turn the conversation back in the direction you wish it to go.

If you relax rather than trying to force a point, you will come across as amiable and a good listener; it's when you insist on pushing a point even when the point in the conversation is less than ideal, that you will be perceived as desperate and manipulative. Not your goal, by the way. Subtly yet powerfully taking control is a true art form unto itself.

Get the agreement

Get the agreement starting with the smaller issues and work your way up. This is self-explanatory. Once you've got the other party agreeing with you on smaller points, they'll be more likely to go the same route on your most important issues.

Establish rapport

Set the pace and lead in the direction you wish it to go. In other words, once you've gotten some agreement, engaged interactivity and rapport, then take charge of the flow/pace of the conversation as you skillfully maneuver it in the direction of your choice by mentioning topics you want to discuss and by asking questions to engage others.

Respectful touch

Periodically, respectfully touch the other person's arm; not too much, simply for emphasis on specific points. Many studies have shown that gently touching a person's arm or shoulder in moderation once in a while opens them up to responding positively to you.

NLP practitioners are among the conversation control "masters" who know the power of using light physical contact to get certain points across. Studies have also shown that people who work in industries where they rely upon tips - i.e., waiters, cab drivers, etc., who respectfully (and just once or twice at most) touch a customer's arm or shoulder often get the best tips!

Know your specific intended outcome

Stays focused, but stay flexible. Once again, you come across as more likeable and easy to talk/work with, when you're not rigid or stubborn about making your points. Keep it lighthearted when the conversation swerves in a different direction; flexibility and humor will go a long way towards others to get back on track when the timing is better.

Casually use provocative examples or questions, to elicit objections, and then overcome them.

Draw out the other person(s) goals/intentions for the conversation by asking them directly

This shows that you're not just an interesting person, but also an interested one. When you appeal to someone's ego by making sure their goals are clearly understood in addition to your own, they are more likely to come over to your way of thinking on the points that matter most to you. Do your best to seek solutions during the course of the conversation which create win-win situation for everyone!

Tie mutual goals into your suggestions

When you've established the other person's goals by drawing them out, point out how parallel their goals and yours are, and how your suggestions can benefit you both.

Ask for what you want, either directly or indirectly

If you don't ask, you don't receive, period! So get over any shyness about asking, no matter what it's for - a promotion, a contract negotiation, a loan at the bank, etc. Rehearse asking in the mirror - record yourself rehearsing, and then later, listen and see if you sound relaxed and confident as you ask.

It's best to record the rehearsal, and then go do something else for at least an hour. This will keep your listening to your rehearsal more objective and honest. It's also good to practice with a family member or a friend who will seriously do some role playing with you and give you an honest feedback.

Utilize small movements/motions to progress your aims.

If you resort to using large gestures, you'll come across as overbearing, or possibly too comedic - not taking the conversation seriously enough. But a little gesture or motion for emphasis can be very effective.

Use T.O.T.E. - Test, Operate, Test, Exit

While this is based on a behavioral model paradigm, it works really well in controlling a conversation as well. This model encourages you to take a trial and error approach to conversation, keep trying different ideas until you find what works best.

When using comparisons in the course of a conversation, the T.O.T.E. model may require a few more test before finally arriving at the Test that is the agreed upon objective, leading to the Exit (successful finish of the conversation).

K.I.S.S. - Keep it Simple, Sovereign

Make your main point and don't elaborate too much. Schedule future conversations to cover other topics. You may be an amazing multi-tasker, but not everyone is, and some people tend to get overwhelmed or confused if you present too much. So scheduling successive follow-up meetings may be your best solution.

The more you train yourself to observe other people's nervous habits (looking at their watch, drumming the table, humming to themselves, etc.) you'll become a star "detective" at figuring out their ideal limits when it comes to their attention spans.

Only answer what you want

Ignore any silly remarks. If you find yourself engaged in a conversation with a smart ass, well, I'll be nice and say "smart aleck," don't allow yourself to be suckered into answering questions you're uncomfortable with. Redirect the conversation by changing the subject, or by using the old technique of answering a question with a question, to redirect it. And if your fellow conversationalist is really good at throwing the bull around, you don't need to get out your shovel - just be the bigger person and ignore their silliness, and refocus the conversation's energy where you need and want it to go.

Stay cool, calm & collected

If the other party tries to rock your emotional state in order to gain control. They might be a master at intimidating you with silly comments or really know how to push all of your buttons (this is especially true of relatives and significant others).

Remember, you are the one in control of your emotions and how long you choose to experience them. After all, nobody is telling you how to feel against your will. If they are, then you need to control more than just a conversation.

Seriously, though, take a few nice, deep, centered breaths anytime you feel yourself sliding down a slippery emotional slope and release any negative feelings. Then turn your valued attention back to what's important in the moment - reaching your goal!

Practice slow, deep diaphragmatic breathing before and during the conversation so you think clearly

This will help you stay calm and levelheaded. Deep breathing is good to practice throughout the conversation. The more oxygenation you send to your lungs and as a result your bloodstream, the more oxygen will flow to your brain, keeping you focused and calm. It's much easier to take control of a conversation from this standpoint than from one of panic and anxiety. BREATHE!

Carefully listen and watch for any unspoken issues and hidden agendas

Don't hesitate to ask for clarity, right then and there. But the more diligent practice you put into mastering mind, the more you'll learn people's "tells" when they are uncomfortable with something you're proposing. Go ahead! Scratch the surface, and ask, "If that scenario you've brought up a few times were to come about, what would be the main advantage for you?" They may be flattered, or possibly offended; hopefully either way, you'll get an answer.

It's better to be direct than to waste everyone's time and energy beating around the bush. A way to "see" someone's resistance is through body language, of course. When someone is crossing their arms across their chest, that's a sure sign they're not open to what you're proposing, or that they're protecting themselves from something they don't want to hear, or perhaps don't understand.

Shift gears, get them to relax and smile, interject some humor about something totally off-topic for just a few seconds to shift the mood, then bring it back where you want the conversation to head.

2: Common Mistakes to Avoid

In this section we'll look at a few common ways people lose control of their minds. We need to be aware of these common mistakes and avoid them completely. We also need to look out for others who are talking because those mistakes on their part represent opportunities for us to step in and take back control.

1. When someone feels nervous, antsy or intimidated right off the bat, they tend to just roll over and relinquish control, thereby giving it to others and allowing them to lead the direction of the conversation.

2. Failure to listen, therefore ignoring key signals from others. Developing your skills as a good listener, as well as a careful observer of body language will go far in helping you maintain or regain control of a conversation.

But if you're so intent on your own objective and you're not really listening to the other party and their needs, it will become painfully obvious to them right away, and more than likely, the conversation will come to a grinding halt, without you getting even one step closer to achieving your objective.

So don't forget there has to be a give and take, much like a game of tennis or ping-pong - you must listen, watch and respond appropriately, not just continuing to smash the ball in a way that doesn't allow the other person to return your serve, so to speak. So "keep your ears on" and your radar attuned to what the other party is seeking, as well as your own goals.

3. Annoying others by ignoring their outcome or values. This pretty much goes hand in hand with not listening. When you ignore someone's desired outcome, or run roughly over their value system, they'll find you to be a rude bore. Now when was the last time you enjoyed talking with a rude bore? Pay attention - LISTEN and respond appropriately. Smile and engage the participation of everyone involved.

4. Fixating on a minor issue and losing sight of the primary goal. This is akin to the old saying that goes, "You can't see the forest for the trees." Don't let one "tree" that might crop up unexpectedly deter you from your most important objective. If it's something that will make the other party more agreeable overall to what you desire, be flexible - negotiate!

5. Answering questions too quickly due to nerves. Many people hastily give an answer without

ruminating upon it for a few moments, or even a minute or two. Never over-promise and under-deliver, if the question has to do with what you're able or willing to do.

If it requires that you do some research prior to giving an informed answer, just be honest and tell them you need some time to come up with the best answer for all concerned. Be sure you write down the point, or make an audio note and record it so they know you're serious. Once you've taken enough time to think it through, whether in that particular conversation, or a bit further down the road, then you can simply redirect the conversation towards your goal and move forward.

6. Letting fear of failure prevent you from going where you want to go. Remember the old mnemonic device - "Fear is False Evidence Appearing Real?" It's quite true. Usually we become afraid of something before it even occurred, or without having all of the details.

Focus on your solution, your goal, rather than on your fear of failure. Going into a conversation knowing what you want and having the confidence to get your point across will help you reach that objective; fear is a "freezer" - it prevents you from moving forward, keeps you stuck, and often causes people to mumble or just give up far too easily.

Be brave, bold and eloquent, while staying respectful to the other party's goals, too. You never know until you try, so go for it!

7. Failure to build a series of small wins before seeking your major outcome or goals. It is so important to cultivate agreement via a series of "baby steps," if you will, prior to diving right in and going after your major goals.

If you're too aggressive about your primary objective and don't give rapport some time to build and strengthen, you'll come across as desperate, pushy or both. Not the way to convince someone to align with you!

Take your time, use some questions to get those "yeses" accumulating, and once the other person is already in the mindset of saying "yes" - then that is the time to go for your big target, but smoothly, and calmly. When you become really good at this, they may not even be aware which one of your goals was your main point. They will just know they like and admire your style, and agree with you.

8. Allowing others to drive will trigger your emotional state. This is a really big one, particularly with relatives, close friends or colleagues. When people you know really well have an innate knowledge of how to "go for your emotional jugular," well, that's just someplace you

don't want to go. You'll lose every time, if you allow this to happen. Remember - nobody is forcing you to feel a particular way; they're not holding a gun to your head telling you how to feel, right? You're in charge of that, no one else.

9. And since forewarned is forearmed, if you're about to engage in a conversation with someone who you know from past experience has pushed all your buttons, simply make sure you take plenty of time to relax and stay focused before your meeting.

You might even imagine a shield or a suit of armor made out of translucent white light that only you can see, protecting you from any type of attack or provocation. It's often especially effective to make sure you have lots of this white light protection around the center of your chest as well as your solar plexus - where those "gut reactions" kicks in.

10. Another great phrase to bear in mind prior to engaging in such conversations is, "What you think of me is none of my business." Know who you are, know thyself, in other words. And don't worry about what the other person may think of you, or how they may have been successfully manipulating you in the past.

You are savvier now. You've taken time to prepare and be on the defensive (quietly, without confrontation). Using humor to redirect a conversation is always another great way to deflect negative feelings and prevent you from getting emotionally unbalanced.

11. Simply giving up when roadblocks appear, rather than focusing on win-wins, and allowing the perceived problems to grow. It's sad but true that a large part of human nature involves unconditional surrender far too early. Giving up when a problem seems insurmountable, rather than mentally taking a giant step back in order to see the big picture and focusing on co-creating solutions and win-wins.

12. Allowing your ego to push you into losing a key point or outcome. Too often, people let their competitive nature (i.e., ego) force them into "pushing beyond the point of no return" when it feels like they have relinquished control of a conversation, or haven't yet achieved their goal.

So if you notice any temptation to allow sarcasm to insidiously come creeping into your side of the talk, it's really a good idea to hold your tongue, take some deep breaths, smile and see if there's a creative way to bring the conversation back around your way. If the other party has viewpoints which you don't share, live and let live; agree to disagree, but don't become combative or confrontational.

Smooth, suave and in control is the key. And even if you don't "win" this particular conversation, at least you won't have burned any bridges, and the other party will still think you're a nice person.

Better that than to remove all doubt from their mind that you're an egomaniac! That only works for dictators, you know - and look what usually winds up happening to most of them.

13. Boring others with too much personal detail; this incites them to stop listening and ultimately, from making a committed agreement. Even if you have a great example story that you feel will help your point come across, perhaps a smarter way to present it would be the old, "You know, a friend of mine had great success when they tried something similar..." and then go ahead with the story.

14. As far as just giving way too much - Limit what you share to the context of the conversation, or what you're comfortable answering when asked any type of personal questions. Keeping a slight air of mystery can sometimes be prudent; and let's face it, unless you're a celebrity, most people don't really want to know all the glorious, tedious details of your life. Focus on what you're aiming to achieve and don't waste anyone's time with unnecessary details.

15. Allowing a fast talker to keep you from getting a word in edgewise. You know, some people are just naturally fast, nonstop talkers. Perhaps this

stems from their own nervousness, or in some cases, loneliness (i.e., you might be the only person who's listened to them for a long time). Or maybe they just have "narcissus ears" and simply are in love with the sound of their own voice.

Whatever the case may be, since you're engaged in conversation with them, you obviously have a desired outcome in mind. If you allow them to continue without giving you the opportunity to bring up your own agenda in any way, shape or form, then you've lost before you've begun. You made sure of that! Here are some ways to get Aunt Cathy to pause for breath and listen to you:

Aunt Cathy: "And then we went to the cutest little store where we found the most adorable little stuffed animal pillows, and oh! That reminds me, my dog Zsa Zsa did the most outrageous thing the other day... .yada, yada, yada... ."

 You (politely interjecting): "Oh, you have a dog named Zsa Zsa? What breed is she?"

Aunt Chatty Cathy: (Possibly startled that someone has actually been paying much attention to what she's been prattling on about) Oh, yes! Zsa Zsa is my toy poodle. She's the love of my life!"

You: "Dogs are great, aren't they? And that's part of why I wanted to have a talk with you."

Just one example: Bear in mind that a very effective way to get the "Aunt Cathy's" in your life to listen to what you have to say is to acknowledge something about their endless stream of words, then get their agreement on a common issue. After that, it's much easier to keep their rapt attention (at least for awhile, as a rule), and focus on what you want to talk about in the first place.

Again, it often comes down to showing the other person that you truly are a nice, considerate person. Don't you prefer to do business, or make plans (whether business or personal) with someone who's nice? And as tempting as it might be to just interrupt their tirade at times and scream, "Don't you ever take a breath or shut up, for gosh sakes?" - that's never going to win you any brownie points, as they say, and certainly not going to further your cause or goal.

So again, exercise patience, breathe deeply, but when that perfect actual two-way communication presents itself, then butting in is not perceived as impolite, but interested. There's a huge difference, isn't there? And wouldn't you agree that getting someone to agree with you is easier if you ask questions once in a while? You get the picture.

3: The Importance of Self-Control

Some scenarios have already been covered about ways to regain control, but this next section is more about things you can do inwardly, to help yourself feel grounded and centered again before you get back in the game with the conversation. A cool thing about these techniques is nobody but you will know you're doing them - they're that subtle. But don't underestimate their value - they can be quite empowering, just when you need it most.

Breathing

The value of taking nice, long, slow diaphragmatic breaths has been discussed a bit, but since "repetition is the mother of skill," it never hurts to touch upon good information again; possibly to revisit it in a slightly different way, or with a bit more detail thrown in for emphasis.

When a baby is first born, they automatically breathe deeply and fully, from the diaphragm muscle. If you doubt this at all, just observe a little baby breathing while it sleeps - its tummy will gently rise and fall with its breath (part of the learning intake process behavior of toddlers).

 So where did we go astray and begin doing more shallow breathing? For most of us, pretty much when we started walking and running. Autonomic breathing seldom happens, at least not while we are awake.

Runners, swimmers, yoga practitioners, students of meditation, and singers learn, or better stated - relearn - the importance of exercising the diaphragm and breathing deeply to create more energy, more stamina, and in the case of singers, more volume and projection.

But if, like the majority of people, you haven't really had the need or opportunity to relearn and practice the art of deep breathing, then it's time!

Not only will taking those long, slow deep breaths calm your nerves and balance your heart rate, it will also clear your mind as more oxygen travels to your bloodstream, and to your brain. The "brain fog" that many modern day multi-taskers suffer from could well become a thing of their past if they were to conscientiously practice deep, diaphragmatic breathing.

Practice it on a frequent basis; it's good for you! After all, it's the way we came into this physical world, breathing deeply and naturally. It's the way our bodies were designed to function.

It's just that in the Western "civilized" world (that can be an oxymoron, but never mind for now), we often are in a hurry to receive instant gratification for just about everything. We forget how to properly do something that is more essential to our existence than eating, drinking, and breathing.

You can go for days without food and water, but not for more than 30 seconds without breath. Ponder that for a bit, and start practicing deep breathing regularly. You'll notice that by breathing deeply while driving, you have more patience with other drivers' behavior, and you're also more clear-headed so you can readily drive defensively - your awareness is sharpened. This is true with many other behaviors as well.

With regard to the importance of deep breathing during a conversation, having built up your stamina and breath support allows you to express yourself easily and eloquently without searching for breath. And if you're a bit overweight, using that diaphragm is also a good way to exercise your waistline area. When you inhale, you should feel your waistline expand.

Singers and others are taught this simple trick to make sure they're breathing deeply and fully:

Place your hands on your waistline so that the tip of your middle finger is lightly touching just above your navel. When you inhale, filling up the diaphragm, the tips of those fingers will be pushed slightly apart as your waistline expands.

Then as you exhale, strive to keep that expansion for as long as you can without running out of breath. That's the exercise part. If you really want to develop that power even more, you can use a three to five pound sandbag. While lying flat on the floor using an exercise mat, place the sandbag in the same position, right around the navel, and breathe in and out, causing the sandbag to gently rise and fall with each deep, rhythmic breath. It's a good way to actually see and feel that you're breathing properly.

So the beauty of all of this - breathing deeply, especially once you've become accustomed to doing it regularly - is something that no one else will detect - that you're doing it in order to stay calm and focused.

Let's take this one step further, shall we? Let's say you've been talking to your Uncle Larry, who has always had a habit of being able to "get your goat," or cause a knee-jerk emotional reaction out of you by pushing your infamous buttons. Well, next time you're around an "Uncle Larry" type, here's another tool you can employ which will go completely undetected, but it will help you tremendously:

As you're taking those nice, slow deep breaths, very slowly and gently, bring your fingertips in to touch the center of your palms, making a very loose, relaxed fist. Do this as you inhale - and hold that breathe for just a few moment.

Notice where you feel the tension in your body, and as you exhale, you're going to release that tension, as well as any negativity. As you exhale, relax your fingertips and point them toward the floor imagining that all of that tension, negativity, and really anything else that is not serving you any good is simply draining right out of your fingers.

This may sound all "airy-faerie" to some of you, but to others who are all too aware that thoughts are things and that we are all made up of energy (quantum physicists are masters of this knowledge and power). Regardless, you'll find that using the finger-flex technique with the deep breathing will help you feel centered quickly and easily, and no one else will be the wiser.

It might also help to think to yourself as you exhale, "Cancel, Cancel" or "Erase, Erase," "Delete, Delete," - whatever word you choose to help your subconscious mind work with you in releasing something that is not serving your best interests.

Then on the next inhalation, think of something that makes you smile for which you are grateful. It's not just the Universe that abhors a vacuum - your subconscious mind does, too! But when you let something go, unless you fill that "void" with something else that's positive, the negative feeling or thought will creep back in, pretty rapidly. That's simply the way our brains are wired. Put this exercise to the test, and I'm willing to wager that it will help you maintain your composure and when heading towards regaining control of a conversation!

Visualization

Using visualization to create your desired outcome is a tool that should never be underestimated, just like the power of breathing. Here are two easy ways to employ it, with regard to regaining control of a conversation.

- Balance your brain!

There's a strip of neurons which connect your left and right brain hemispheres. This strip is called the corpus callosum. This arched band of nerve fibers allows both sides of your brain to communicate.

Most people process life and its experiences more with one side or the other of the brain - i.e., artistic, creative individuals tend to be more right-brained, while scientists, accountants, and other generally logical, analytically minded folks lean more toward left-brain dominance. You'll be amazed how good this left/right brain balancing technique makes you feel.

Shower Power! Mentally tune into that corpus callosum. As you inhale, imagine it filling up with brilliant white light that is filled with calm wisdom and healing, from Divine Source, if you believe in that, or simply from Universal Energy, if you're more comfortable with that paradigm.

Hold the breath for a count of 3, and then as you exhale, silently tell yourself, "Shower, shower, shower," and imagine that beautiful white light flowing equally over both sides of your remarkable brain - still the most amazing computer on earth.

Do this 2 or 3 times until you feel yourself calm and rebalanced, and then you'll be able to smoothly and intelligently find the means of taking control of the conversation again.

And as a bonus - once again, no one else has a clue of the empowering tool you just used. But they'll notice you have more energy, a light in your eyes and a sense of calm and strength - always a good place to be when making your point!

Visualize it happening

Before you make your move to regain control, take a few moments to tune into what it will feel, sound and look like. It's as simple as that. Athletes who visualize successfully completing their event or other sports activities have been hooked up to electrodes which measure their muscle response while they're visualizing.

And behold, the same muscle groups' fire while they're simply running the event in their mind! So there's scientific evidence that visualization can help create your success.

It's another way of rehearsing for your smash hit play called "Life!" Or in this case, "Regaining Control of a Conversation in a Scene from the Play Called Life."

Try it - it's free!

4: How to Prepare

Old adages have been around for decades, and in some cases centuries, for good reason. It is because they are often infused with sage wisdom. For instance, are you familiar with the one that goes, "An ounce of prevention is worth a pound of cure"? Well, that applies to the art of controlling minds. When you take the time to prepare in advance for an upcoming scheduled meeting, you're better equipped to avoid pitfalls, or to know how to handle expected objections, etc. By practicing some of the following tips and techniques, you'll build your confidence level, be perceived as a master of conversation, and more often than not, be able to reach your goals. So let's get started!

1. Create your game plan - clarify your goals before you even set up the conversation.

Basically, make sure you know beyond a shadow of a doubt what your end objective, your best case scenario outcome from the conversation is. Examine both sides of the equation here - in other words, look at how your goal will be mutually beneficial so you can point out to the other person how conjoint agreement will bring benefit to them - not just to you. This needs to be a sincere benefit, not just so many words, so do some good pre-planning.

2. Visualize/rehearse the meeting in your mind; even go so far as to act it out, possibly even video tape or record it so you have the most accurate picture of how you'll look and sound.

The camera doesn't lie, and this is a technique often employed by actors and public speakers so they can actually put themselves in the audience's shoes, or in your case, the other conversationalist's shoes.

Stay objective as you watch the playback - if you didn't know the person on camera, would you trust them? Why or why not? If there are areas for improvement (trust me, there always is), what is required to make those improvements?

For example, if it's making better eye contact - then you need to practice making better eye contact. It's that simple. No one likes talking to someone with "shifty" eyes, or who is so self-conscious they are always looking around and never directly at you. Now, practicing in the mirror or on camera is good, but putting it into practical application is superb! And those with whom you're practicing don't even have to know they're helping you. How, you ask? It's very simple.

Make eye contact, at least more than you've normally been comfortable with, with everyone you meet. The cashier at the grocery store; people on the bus or subway; strangers on the street - don't stare, just nod and smile. Not everyone will play along, especially complete strangers, but you'll be surprised - most people will!

Sometimes people walking down the street are feeling as lonely or self-conscious as you might be. A friendly smile, eye contact and a nod might just make their day, and it puts you one step closer to building up your own confidence, so don't be shy!

Once you become more comfortable with making eye contact, then progress on to a line or two of small talk, particularly if you're good with making humorous remarks. Laughter is very healing, and even a comment made by a witty stranger can help someone have a better day.

Practice makes perfect, so seize every opportunity you have to improve in the areas that need fine-tuning. Chances to practice are out there, available to all of us each and every day. Make use of them, and have fun along the way. It doesn't have to be deadly serious. In fact, it is much better if it's not.

3. Take time before the meeting to get yourself centered and focused. Allow plenty of time to get ready before-hand and avoid anything or anyone that might cause you to become emotionally out of balance. This is VERY important, especially if the upcoming meeting is very important to you. You may be asking for a promotion/raise, a loan or investment opportunity, a key turning point in a relationship, etc.

Again, the rehearsing beforehand can prove to be invaluable, so don't discount that, but simply making sure you create the time in advance to prepare is extremely important.

Also taking every precaution possible to make sure that you have a good night's sleep prior to the meeting is an excellent form of preparation. By doing this in addition to taking a few minutes just before the meeting, you go into it feeling rested, calm, vibrant, and focused on your agenda rather than emotionally, physically or mentally exhausted.

4. Take care of your physical needs

Stay hydrated. It is amazing how dry one's mouth and throat can become while talking. Coffee is a diuretic, so if you're meeting at Starbuck's or another coffee place, make sure you have a glass or bottle of water handy, in addition to any Java.

If your throat has a bit of a tickle, take some cough drops with you. Better that you nurse one of those and be able to continue talking than to cough and hack your way through the conversation. If "nature calls" during the meeting, don't be shy about excusing yourself.

It is very important that you feel comfortable and relaxed throughout the meeting. All of this is just good common sense, obviously, but go ahead and put it into practice. It will all work to your advantage, so why not do it?

5: Getting Real with Yourself

Okay, it's time to "get real" with yourself; unbridled self-honesty is called for in order to become as effective at controlling minds as possible. If you already know what your strengths are from your past success (where you've held or regained control of a mind), write down those strengths that have worked.

On the opposite side of the coin, if you're aware of your weaknesses, then you need to write those down as well. In fact, those are actually more important to know and understand than your strengths. You probably already know a few of those weaknesses. Do any of these sound familiar?

- You find yourself feeling short of breath when you feel like you've been put on the spot or when the conversation's control has flipped to the other person.

- Your palms get sweaty, and perhaps you're perspiring in other places more than usual as well.

- You tend to stammer or feel tongue-tied when the other person assumes control.

- You let yourself become easily distracted during the course of the conversation, and then never manage to bring it back around to your true agenda, thereby missing your goal altogether.

There may be others, but these are a few common ones. And you know what? We have now covered several tools with just a bit of diligent practice on your part, can help you balance, correct and overcome ANY of these weaknesses, as well as many other reactions or "spots" you might find yourself in, during a conversation.

None of these are life-threatening, so just relax. Practice, practice, practice, remember? It's not just the way to "get to Carnegie Hall" - it is something that's required in any facet of life in order to master a skill - including being an effective communicator and controller of minds.

6: How to Control Difficult People

No one likes dealing with difficult people, but sometimes the task is required. In order to control difficult people, you need to be in control of yourself and your stress level first. For people in high stress jobs such as retail, taking the time to relax and re-center themselves can help provide the emotional energy for dealing with such individuals. People who do not take the time to refresh and recharge themselves may not be able to handle stressful situations of any kind as well as they otherwise would.

Effects of stress

Stress is a serious issue that has physical, mental and emotional consequences. It can never be entirely avoided because it is a normal reaction to dealing with difficult situations in everyday life. However, it can be dealt with by taking time to consciously relax.

The effects of stress are cumulative to a certain extent. People who work in stressful environments all week are usually much more stressed out on Thursday than on Monday. The weekend provides a chance to rest and recover that the shorter, overnight break between workdays does not offer.

Stress and emotional energy

Everyone has had a moment in their lives where they just could not deal with a situation any longer. Usually, the reaction to reaching this point is quite dramatic, involving yelling, tears, or stomping off in a huff. In most cases, it is not the specific situation that caused the person to reach their breaking point, but the amount of emotional energy they had when they got into the situation.

People have longer "fuses" when they are under less stress. Individuals each have their own unique ability to deal with emotionally stressful situations and some are naturally more tolerant of them than others. However, anyone can increase their ability to deal with stressful situations by consciously relieving stress.

Reactions to difficult people

The opposite reaction to the dramatic "breaking point" screaming or crying is to shut down. This often happens when people are involved in stressful situations within their own families or in other areas of life where they cannot get away.

Shutting down can lead to making unhealthy decisions simply to please the difficult person. This is because making the healthier decision would require fighting and fighting requires energy.

Relieving stress can allow people in these situations to build up their reserves and fight for their own needs to be met. It takes more emotional energy initially but can result in a better situation overall.

People who find themselves shutting down may need to remove themselves from the situation until they have recharged their batteries. Then they can fight for their needs.

Relieving stress

Ways of relieving stress are unique to individuals. Some common activities that people use for stress relief include physical exertion, social gatherings, quiet time spent with friends and family, creative endeavors and much more. Generally, anything that leaves someone feeling more relaxed when they are finished will be considered a method of stress relief.

As you deal with difficult people, be aware of your own stress levels. If you sense that you are under a lot of stress, remove yourself from the situation. Ask someone else for help to deal with the difficult person so you can reduce your stress and regain your emotional energy. Being calm within yourself is the first step towards successfully dealing with difficult people.

7: How to Control Annoying People

One standard personality that can be difficult to control is the one who seems to annoy you from the moment they walk in the room. It is easy to lose your cool when someone's nagging personality is regularly annoying you. However, there are a few tips that you can follow to avoid letting them get under your skin.

Listen to them

With some annoying, nagging people, you have little to no need to interact with them on a daily basis. Others, however, have job functions that overlap or intertwine with yours in some way, so it is necessary to listen to their nagging.

In most cases, when someone is nagging you, they have a strong desire to relay some seemingly important message to you, and they will persist in trying to communicate this message until you affirm that you have heard and understood it.

Therefore, pause and listen to the message fully. Give this person your full, undivided attention, and use effective communication skills to affirm that you have heard their message. This may mean saying something along the lines of, "I understand what you have said." This will help them feel that they have been heard and move along quicker.

Make sound decisions

There is a difference between listening to and understanding what someone is saying and following their instructions. Some people may be so irritated with a person that their first inclination is to immediately deny any request that the person has made.

However, it is important to always make sound, impartial decisions even when you are feeling annoyed. Therefore, while listening to the person, try to consider what the fair, impartial solution is.

Be firm

Once you have made up your mind, be firm in your resolve. If your decision is counter to this person's wishes, denying their request or failing to follow their instructions may result in continued nagging.

Simply state your decision, and offer a small explanation regarding the reason for your decision. It is not necessary or beneficial to engage in a back-and-forth debate about the topic if you have heard the request, and you have made a fair decision.

Create space

To avoid being subject to continued nagging, it is often necessary to walk away from someone who is nagging. You can and should do this politely. After you have stated what you need to say, simply tell the person that you have a phone call to take.

Dealing with a nagging, annoying person can make you miserable, and your response to their behavior can reflect poorly on you rather than them.

8: How to Control a Bully

Controlling a bully or any person who is dominating and overbearing can be overwhelming. There are a few tips available to help you become more assertive while standing your ground. It is important to learn how to stand up for yourself to get rid of the bullies you are dealing with in your everyday life.

Assess the situation and avoid blaming yourself

When you feel as if you are a victim of bullying or an overly-assertive personality, it is important to understand that the abuse is not your fault or even triggered by you, but it is an issue for the bully. Detaching yourself from any blame when dealing with a bully can help you find a sense of relief, while you become more assertive yourself.

Assess why you believe you are being bullied, and try to find ways to avoid the bully altogether within your home or your workplace. This helps distance you from the bully emotionally and physically. By ignoring the bully and also disregarding any self-blame and negative emotions, the bully will likely move on to someone who is considered "weaker" or an easier target in their eyes.

Use kindness

Use kindness to help with deterring a bully if you are not one for confrontation. Although avoiding the bully and speaking kindly to the bully at all times may not help, it may help you to feel a sense of peace from the situation.

When you detach yourself from any negative emotions the bully frequently evokes it will allow you to feel less stressed. Smile, nod and agree and simply walk away from someone who is being too assertive, aggressive or who is acting as a bully.

Presenting yourself as assertive

Stand Tall. Improve your posture. Make direct eye contact with bullies, or those with assertive personalities. This will also help you to become more confident yourself. When you present yourself as assertive, you are able to give off confidence that will often be avoided by potential bullies and those who are too domineering.

You can also improve your assertiveness and confidence by practicing conversations and responses with family members and friends. Avoid showing any weakness in your facial expressions and emotions, even when you are provoked by rude people.

Keep calm

When you are confronted by a bully or a person who enjoys dominating conversations and being assertive, stay as calm as possible to avoid showing that you are intimidated. Avoiding a display of emotions will inform the bully you are just as assertive. Instead, keep a "poker face" without any emotion if you are being taunted, yelled at or in severe cases, berated. Also, be sure to report someone who is being overly aggressive, especially when you are in a workplace together.

Bullies and dominant people do not go away as we leave elementary school. They are all around us. As you become more assertive and gain confidence, a bully will not see you as an easy victim. They will be more likely to leave you alone. Use these strategies to regain your power around a bully or a dominant personality.

9: How to Control a Victim Personality

People with both a victim personality type and a blaming personality type will often make an effort to avoid taking personal responsibility for their life. A person with a victim personality may feel as though life's circumstances or the actions of others have resulted in their own misfortune.

They are a victim, and they may want you to pity them and give them special benefits as a result. Those with a blaming personality may seek advice from you or others in an effort to avoid having any personal responsibility in the outcome of their life. Dealing with both types of individuals can be emotionally exhausting. Learning how to deal with these individuals is imperative to finding happiness in your own life.

Recognizing the behavior

Many people who have these personality types do not fully understand what they are doing. While some may be consciously trying to manipulate you, others may wholeheartedly believe that the world is out to get them or that their life's circumstances are not their fault. At first, you can try to help this person to recognize this behavior. Ask them questions that may lead them on a path of self-discovery. While doing this, be sure that the questions are not pointed or blamed. The right questions may not result in immediate change, but they can ignite a small spark that can ultimately lead to self-awakening over time.

Enabling change

There is a possibility that you may actually be enabling this person's behavior to continue. Take time to consider how you react when this person plays the victim card or seeks your advice.

Do you rush to the aid of a friend with a victim personality, or do you offer the blaming personality type friend with the advice they are seeking? It is important that you learn how to change your behavior so that you can elicit change in your friend. Your own reactions may be enabling the behavior. Try to help them think of ways that they can solve the problem, instead of complaining and blaming.

Don't feel responsibility

Your friend's personality may evolve over time, or they may continue to be the same for the rest of their life. Either way, it is important for you to learn that you are not responsible for this person's care and well-being.

You can lend an ear when needed, as a good friend would. However, you should avoid feeling any emotional attachment to this person's life events or challenges. Understand what events you actually are responsible for and what events are beyond your control. Ultimately, it is up to your friend to learn how to live their own life while you live your life.

Dealing with those who have a victim or blaming personality can be challenging on many levels. While you may want to be a caring friend, it is important that you identify the areas that you can actually provide assistance with, as well as your own behaviors that may be enabling this behavior. In some instances, it may be necessary for you to make personal changes in your behavior. Then you can expect to see changes in your friend.

10: How to Control your Boss

Some bosses are great to work for. While they may expect you to work hard, they also make reasonable expectations and give you the freedom to find a balance between work and your personal life.

Others, however, are overbearing, demanding and often set unrealistic expectations that can drive you crazy. If you work for a boss who falls into the latter group, you will need to find a way to deal with this boss in a respectful, reasonable way.

Effective communication skills

One of the best steps that you can take when working with a difficult boss is to utilize effective communication skills. If your boss is the type of person who likes to provide you with half-instructions or change instructions in the middle of a project, bring a notepad with you to each meeting you have with them.

Jot down any instructions they provide. Before you leave their presence, repeat the instructions that you have written down. This will accomplish two things. First, it provides your boss with the ability to add to the instructions before you begin working on the project.

Second, it makes you look as though you are diligent and committed to following through on their instructions perfectly. It may be wise to follow up with your boss about the status of a project several times to ensure that your work meets their expectations.

Set limits

It is important to understand your rights as a worker and to establish limits regarding your work hours and free time. Unless you have a position where you are required to be on-call, it is not reasonable or appropriate for your boss to call you during your off-hours regarding work-related manners.

Let these calls go to voice mail. Listen to the messages, and send a quick text message to your boss saying that you are out-of-pocket. You will gladly talk to them about the issue bright and early on your next scheduled work day. Furthermore, avoid being roped into staying after hours if possible. Keep in mind that once you have established the precedence of staying late or working on the weekends, this may become an expectation.

Maintain distance

It is important to maintain distance from your boss as much as possible. This is a person who you must work with and must take instructions from, but this does not mean that you need to hang out with the person all of the time.

You can decrease your annoyance with this person and keep your blood pressure lower by working on your own as much as possible. Also, avoid extracurricular activities with your boss outside of the office. If you are permitted to, consider working from home as much as possible.

Do what you need to do in order to keep your job and don't make yourself appear too aloof. However, distance can be healthy when dealing with someone who irritates you.

Many people will deal with a difficult boss at one point or another. How you manage your relationship with this person will ultimately affect your sanity and your ability to keep your job. Follow these strategies to control your difficult boss more effectively.

11: How to Control a Difficult Customer

Whether you work in an office building, or in retail, at one point or another, you will have to deal with a difficult customer. They are agitated and upset and you happened to be the lucky employee who stepped up to help them.

In order to control a difficult customer, you must first remain calm and avoid taking the anger of the customer personally. It's difficult to solve problems under stress. It's important for the customer service representative to recognize that the anger being expressed is the result of the situation and the customer's frustration.

The next step is to acknowledge the customer's anger and frustration. This is a crucial step. In many cases being listened to and acknowledged is the main thing that angry customers are seeking.

Customer service representatives can let the customer know that they are being heard as well as ensure that they understand the nature of the problem correctly. You can do this by repeating the main part of the problem back to the customer and confirming its accuracy.

It's important to apologize to the customer without offering excuses or trying to shift blame, even if there are good excuses and blame belongs elsewhere. These initial responses will defuse the anger of many customers.

Next, it's important to identify whether the customer wants the problem solved, wants compensation or wants both. Ideally, one could provide both, but in some cases, such as a gift failing to arrive on time or a bowl of soup spilled on the lap of a diner, it is no longer possible to rectify the initial issue.

When at all feasible, however, the customer service representative should focus on solving the problem as described by the customer.

Compensation can be tricky. Customers who are skilled negotiators may already have a form of compensation in mind. This can actually make one's job easier if the compensation is a reasonable one such as a restaurant meal for unsatisfactory food or service. However, the customer may demand unreasonable compensation. In this case one must be diplomatic in negotiating with the customer to agree to a reasonable amount of compensation that the customer still feels is adequate.

It's still a good idea, though, to ask the customer what action would make them happy. The customer should begin to feel as though you are no longer an adversary but an ally in working to solve the problem.

The customer service representative might use inclusive language like "we" to discuss the issue such as "What can we do to resolve this?" A customer who demands impossible solutions or compensation should be reassured that you are doing everything in one's power to solve the issue. Also state that you will continue working with the customer until the issue is resolved to everyone's satisfaction.

Throughout the interaction, it's important to continue treating the customer like a fellow human being. Empathy is vital. Often, the anger of a customer comes from feeling powerless.

Depending on the nature of the problem and what is at stake, it may also arise from understandable fears and frustrations. Putting oneself in the customer's shoes and working to fix the situation from that viewpoint can provide valuable insight and the very best customer service.

With these strategies, you can hope to diffuse the anger of a difficult customer and help solve their problems. As you work together with the customer, you can change a negative experience with your company into a positive one.

12: How to Control a Difficult Family Member

Most people have at least one family member who they deem to be difficult to get along with. They just seem to push your buttons, or perhaps you have a history with them that is hard to overcome. Finding a way to deal with this particular family member is critical to minimizing stress for you and others at family functions and other events.

Avoid confrontation when possible

Many difficult people are either confrontational in nature or may easily turn even the slightest comment that you make into a major issue. Confrontations with family members are never pleasant. They can easily cause stress and tension with other family members too.

Someone will have to make the decision to be the "bigger person" to avoid World War III erupting in your family, and this may fall onto your shoulders. It is important to understand what sets this person off so avoid being confrontation. While you should not be expected to walk on eggshells around your family, some reservation around this person can go a long way toward keeping the peace.

When you do have a confrontation

While your best efforts may help you to minimize the possibility of a confrontation, you may still find yourself involved in a heated argument with this person from time to time. It may be wise to remove yourself from the situation as soon as possible so that regrettable words muttered in the heat of the moment can be avoided.

Once you have calmed down, consider making an effort to smooth things over. You may not want to apologize if you did nothing wrong. However, taking a few minutes to remind your family member that you love them and that you regret the argument may help you to get over this rough patch.

Establish boundaries

One of the reasons that you may find your family member to be difficult to deal with may relate to boundaries. For example, the person may regularly say things that you find inappropriate or undermine your authority to your kids.

It is important that you clearly state what your boundaries are. Calmly but firmly point out the specific times when you believe your family member has crossed the lines that you have established. It may take them some time, but eventually, they may learn how to treat you how you want to be treated.

While these steps may help you to deal more effectively with a difficult family member, there are times when the best medicine is space. Perhaps you will choose only to see them at family events, or only to speak with them on the phone occasionally.

Reflect on the times and instances when this person has angered you and try to avoid those types of situations. This is a person who you may love but who you may not get along well with due to different personality types.

Accepting that you may not get along with every member of your family is ok as well. Because of this, it may be best to establish some distance between the two of you. Controlling a difficult family member can be stressful and must be handled with sensitivity.

As you incorporate these practices, remember that many do not want to abandon a family member, but healthy boundaries may also be necessary.

13: How to Control Yourself

We all have our own difficult personality traits that tend to flare up inside of us when faced with conflict. Achieving goals and maintaining an emotional balance is possible when you recognize your personality strengths and limits.

Difficult personality traits can be limiting and put you at a disadvantage when faced with conflict. You will want to recognize and manage these personal demons when it comes to confronting challenges.

Anger and aggression

Aggressive behavior can detract from the point you are trying to make and may lead to dismissal. When you feel anger coming on, redirect your mind, or, if possible, walk away from the situation.

Passive-aggressive behavior

Falling into passive-aggressive actions may become another emotional contagion. Unfortunately, you may not recognize you are even acting in this manner.

Therapy can help in these circumstances so that you can avoid this destructive behavior. If you find that your feelings often are out of balance with your work and resentment becomes a constant theme of your day, then you may need to look into other career opportunities.

Critical/judgmental behavior

Being the source of constant criticism and judgments of others can lapse into sabotage for yourself and others. This type of difficult behavior is ripe for an exercise described by executive educator Marshall Goldsmith. His exercise starts with the sentence, "When I get better at..." and calls for you to finish the thought multiple ways to find the benefits of improving some aspect or behavior in your life.

One person in Goldsmith's exercise found that saying, "When I become less judgmental," started him on a path toward discovering the benefits of letting go of judgmental thought patterns.

Try this exercise on your own to determine what difficult personality traits you may have. Then take some time to reflect on how you can control yourself in conflict situations and what you can do to improve it.

14: Body Language Tips

The room is silent. Nobody has moved an inch. Yet, so much has been said. How can this be? The secret language of body language is at work.

What if I told you that the most critical aspect of controlling minds doesn't require any words at all? Body language transmits cues, emotions, and implications that speak volumes above any conventional conversation.

Knowing how to not only read other people's body language, but to parlay your own body language into a subliminal message, is a powerful tool. It can communicate your feelings as well as influence the emotional reactions of others.

Body language is a terrific indicator for attraction, approval, and influence. Body language can also be used to gauge levels of aggression in other people. Being able to detect the subtle, and sometimes not so subtle, indicators of aggressive feelings can give you an edge in interpersonal relationships and business negotiations.

A road map to aggressive body signals

There is a very specific group of movements that reveals aggression. The signals often take place throughout the entire body, and also show up on a person's face.

These facial signals include tight lips, pursed lips, and snarling lips. Eyes that keep a rigid stance for a prolonged period of time without the usual blinking or looking away also indicate aggression.

Another characteristic is squinting. This is a technique which subconsciously prevents other people from knowing where the aggressor is looking. It then gives them the evolutionary benefit of the element of surprise when they attack their adversary.

Hands that are clenched into fists or lowered towards the hips and spread out indicates aggressive behavior. The person is posturing themselves for remaining balanced should they launch an attack.

So once you have identified body language as being aggressive, what can you do to diffuse the situation before it escalates into a confrontation? The answer may require you to use your head, but the truth is that it's all in your feet.

Back up

Picture a game board featuring a map of the world like in the classic game of Risk. Moving your game pieces closer and closer to the opposing player's piece is a signal of aggression.

The last thing you want to do in real life is instigate aggression by moving yourself too close to the other person's territory. Being in close proximity to a difficult person or angry person, even to comfort them will serve as an act of aggression as if to challenge them. Actions like a gentle pat on the shoulder or a hug at the wrong moment will be seen as a strict violation of personal space.

A calm face

In difficult situations, many of us unknowingly reveal our frazzled state by body language like keeping a clenched jaw. If you want to convey a sense of serenity in order to diffuse an aggressive situation, start by relaxing the muscles on your face. Try and display a subtle smile.

Your eyes should remain steady and focused, but not so focused that you appear to be staring the other person down. Avoid darting your eyes, which reveals a frightened state or nervousness.

If there is more than one person in the room, make sure your eyes rove enough to include all of them in your speech. A focused, but non-staring, gaze displays that you are present and attentive without being hostile.

Posture yourself for peace

Good posture shows that you are in control of yourself. Your head should be held high with your shoulders back at all times. Bending your head at the neck can give off an indication that you are frightened, making you appear to be an easy target.

Play the right hand

Hand movements are also a tell-tale sign of what your emotions truly are in a given situation. Quick gestures of the hand can make you appear out of control or nervous. A steady hand gives off an aura of coolness. Avoidance behaviors such as picking lint from your clothing or rubbing your hands can make you appear weak.

It's important to not only be conscious of what you're saying with your words, but what your body language is telling them. As you send out a message of calm and confidence, you will help diffuse the situation. By reading their body language, you may also be able to protect yourself from an unwanted attack.

15: Dealing with Naysayers

Trying to improve yourself can be a difficult task. It is even more strenuous when needless obstacles block your path. The most common roadblock comes from those closest to you. The naysayers, those that offer every difficulty you might encounter. We have all dealt with these personality types. The ones that attempt to convince you of your failure, offering nothing in the way of support; they live to plant seeds of doubt in your mind.

How often have you enthusiastically shared an idea with a friend or family member only to have them tell you that you will not succeed? They project their own fears on to you and sit back waiting for a chance to say, "I told you so." If not dealt with immediately, these outbursts of negativity affect the way you think. An uncle may own a stick-shift car and when you say that you would like to learn, you are told it is too difficult for you to learn.

They are simply placing the idea in your mind that you would not be competent to learn to drive a standard vehicle. Or the business owner who tells colleagues of their speculations for expansion, only to be told that it is the wrong time, a bad economy, stormy weather, or a multitude of excuses as to why their plans are destined to failure.

Dealing with these barriers can be a treacherous trail. They will act as a malignancy that may destroy your aspirations. The easiest way to counteract their negativity is to identify their difficulties and request a solution.

If an aunt tells you that your new diet will not work. Repeat their disapproval back to them. "You do not think the plan I am contemplating will work for me?" Wait for them to acknowledge your statement.

Once acknowledged, ask them to suggest a better idea. This will cause them to pause, as difficult people are often dismissed. They are permitted to voice their negativity, without ever being put in a position to defend their criticisms. By acknowledging their observations, you will catch them off guard. This will make it easier to identify if their intentions are questionable or logical.

It could be that they are just trying to denigrate you, or they have a keen proficiency to assess risk. It is important that you determine their motivation before removing them from your life.

If you determine that the person is unable to be part of a solution, then logic will tell you, they are part of the problem. Abruptly ending the relationship may result in hard feelings.

It is best to avoid a separation that results in animosity, as you may continue to deal with the individual's difficulties in the future. By making them feel awkward in their statements however, the individual will slowly seek out others that are more susceptible to their maliciousness. With no aspirations of their own, they attempt to dissuade any others from improving their life's circumstances.

These are the people that you want to slowly distance yourself from. You can start by simply not answering their calls, or stop inviting them over. If you happen to see them at a social event, you can say hi, but do not need to dwell long in their presence.

Over time, your connection with them will fade. Once you succeed in distancing the difficult people from your life, you can enjoy the pursuance of your dreams unhindered.

16: The importance of mindfulness

Here are the basic but essential purposes of mindfulness and how they can benefit a person's life.

To improve concentration

Being mindful is being able to focus and concentrate, and when you are able to focus and concentrate, you are able to do all your tasks and activities well and you will achieve great results.

Mindfulness is aimed to achieve an improvement on your focus and concentration since it encourages a person to live by the present and to the reality displayed in front of you.

For instance, if there is work to be done and projects are due, if you are mindful, you are able to concentrate on your projects and work because you focus on what you have to do at the moment.

To obtain wisdom easily

Mindfulness is also aimed for the achievement of wisdom and knowledge without obstacles. For instance, if you are inside a class or a seminar, you will not be able to absorb all the knowledge and the wisdom imparted by the instructor or the speaker if you are absent-minded and you do not focus on what is being discussed.

However, if you are mindful, wisdom and knowledge can easily penetrate to your mind and this could benefit your work, your studies and your overall life in a positive way.

To relieve physical stress and prevent heath issues

Mindfulness is also aimed for the purpose of eradicating stress from your life. The world is full of stress-triggers but since mindfulness encourages you and helps you think of the present reality, stress can be reduced and relieved.

Now, stress is one of the main causes of several diseases like high blood pressure. When you are mindful, you eliminate stress and when you eliminate stress, you are also able to prevent serious health issues from arising, thereby keeping you healthy physically.

To eliminate worries

Mindfulness is aimed for the elimination of worry in your daily life. Worry is one great factor that can cause stress and jeopardize your health not only physically, but mentally.

However, if you are mindful or if you know how to practice mindfulness, you are usually trained to focus on the present things and to view things as they are and without judgment.

Since you won't have to think of other things from the past or future, there is nothing to worry about, so you can give your body a good rest, peace to your mind, and happiness to your soul.

To eliminate depression and other mental disorders

Mindfulness is said to be a mental state of focus and concentration, as well as awareness of the present realities. Since it deals mainly with the mind, it is also aimed for the elimination of mental disorders such as depression, anxiety disorders, etc.

For instance, if you are depressed over something, ignoring that mental state could give worst results, like giving you a nervous breakdown. But since mindfulness encourages meditation and freeing the mind from worries that lead to depression, these mental disorders can successfully be eliminated allowing you to live a happier life.

To banish communication gaps

Communication gaps are usually the main causes of misunderstandings. But mindfulness is a state that is aimed to bridge these gaps. Mindfulness can do this because it is the state of paying attention.

Naturally, when you focus and pay attention to the person talking, whether it is your boss, your wife, your parents, etc. you will be able to understand what he or she is saying. Therefore, if it is a task you are supposed to do, you can perform it exactly how your boss wants it or how your parents want it, leading to harmonious relationships.

To banish relationship problems

While communication gaps can cause misunderstandings, misunderstanding are the main culprits of broken and strained relationships; whether with your boss, wife, parents, friends, etc.

The state of being mindful can prevent problems and fix broken relationships because mindfulness not only encourages attentiveness and total awareness, but also encourages viewing things as they are without passing judgment.

This means you are able to absorb the circumstances and understand them. When you understand situations and circumstances despite their negative nature, you avoid misunderstanding and fights with your boss, wife, friends, parents, etc., leading to the avoidance of relationship strains and problems.

To be non-judgmental

It is actually human nature to be judgmental and to put meaning on everything around them. Whether it's an object, a situation or happening, people will judge, and usually they judge the past and even the future of that certain situation.

However, mindfulness is aimed to focus on the present moment as it encourages the viewing of things as they are and not digging up the past and predicting the future. People are trained to be non-judgmental but they will accept and absorb everything without passing judgment.

To get a hold of yourself or your sanity

Many people who experience depression as well as other psychological problems usually are not able to maintain their sanity and get a hold of their emotions. That is why they usually give up and break down. Reality will always have some things that could make a person depressed and worry, but being mindful can help a person keep his or her sanity despite all the stressors and depression-triggers.

It is aimed to let you live one day at a time, solving problems for the day and not to worry about problems that have not arrived. With this, you are able to prevent a surge of problems that that can trigger too much depression allowing you to live and think well despite the not-so-good things happening around you.

To live a happy and contented life

Mindfulness is also aimed for people to achieve a happy and contented life. Nobody wants to be lonely and live a life of misery and discontentment. If you are practicing mindfulness in your daily life, you live for the present and this can train you to be contented with your life. You can be happy because you learned to banish negative vibes and stressors that disrupted your way of life.

Achieving mindfulness

You would never achieve mindfulness if you are not truly convinced that such state exists and that it can be achieved. Only when you believe this first step, mindfulness can be successfully achieved.

Learn all about it

Get to know what this state of mind is all about, its pros and cons and why you need to achieve it. Once you get to know what mindfulness is and its importance, you'll see the significance of it in your life and you start to embrace it.

Ask other people for testimonies and opinions

If you know of some people who are practicing mindfulness, you can ask for their opinions and testimonies as to how mindfulness benefitted their lives and if it is really an effective strategy to be happy.

Asking other people for their experiences will give you more insight as to what mindfulness is and you'll get a clearer picture. You will be encouraged to embrace its importance since the views you have actually comes from people who have used it.

Know your goals and your problem areas

In other words, check your life and your needs with regard to physical, mental, emotional and spiritual health. What problems are you encountering regarding these areas in your life? Do you want mental improvement? Do you want emotional relief from depression and stress? Look into these things and try to compare how mindfulness can bring positive results to these problem areas in your life. When you see the results mindfulness can bring, you will be more encouraged to try.

Apply the nothing-to-lose mindset

When it comes to practicing mindfulness, you will not be required to go on a diet or to give something. Therefore, there is nothing to lose. When you have this mindset, you will be encouraged to try and embrace the importance of mindfulness and see if it really can work for you. When you start practicing mindfulness, you are now increasing your chances to achieve success.

Meditation

Meditation is an effective way to achieve mindfulness because it let you get in touch with your mind and inner self. Since meditation is focusing and concentrating on yourself and not the outside world and its distractions, you are able to pay close attention to reality at the moment, helping you master mindfulness.

Go somewhere quiet

Choose a place where it is peaceful and quiets so you can practice meditation. It will help you concentrate.

Decide what meditation position to apply

This means that whether you want to sit on the floor or sit on a chair, your position should be just comfortable enough. You don't want to get too comfortable as you might feel sleepy and it will hamper meditation.

Close your eyes

When meditating for mindfulness, it is advisable to close your eyes. This will help you focus quickly as a beginner since you won't be able to see distracting things around you.

Be wary of your breathing

As a beginner, your starting focus point for meditation is your breathing. Start by listening to yourself inhale and then exhale and focus on the rhythm. This will get rid of distracting thoughts that could hinder your to meditation.

Be wary of the sounds around you as well as your thoughts

When meditating, you can't help but hear sounds around you. Do not let sounds be a distraction to you but make it another focal point to meditate better. It's the same when thoughts pop up. You welcome these thoughts but keep it calm.

Do this for 20 minutes

Do the meditation for at least 20 minutes a day. Meditating will help you know how to control your mind and your focus despite distractions.

Advanced tips

Many people practice mindfulness, but not all of them succeed in achieving this state of mind.

Achieving mindfulness can be a challenge, but here are some good if you want to successfully achieve mindfulness and ensure your efforts are not in vain.

Know the obstacles to achieving mindfulness

What makes the achievement of mindfulness a real challenge are the obstacles you will meet along the way.

One, achieving mindfulness takes time. It is not achieved instantly and sometimes you will reach the point of giving up before you can actually achieve and master it. Two, achieving mindfulness takes a bit of effort on your part. You'll need to try your best even if your best isn't good enough yet. And three, there will always be distractions and these distractions can really discourage you or shift your thoughts towards achieving mindfulness. Just when you thought you are succeeding something happens and snatches your mindfulness away.

So, as a tip, it is important to know what these obstacles are. When studying mindfulness, do not just learn the benefits but be prepared for obstacles that may come your way. And when you know what to expect, you will also learn to avoid these obstacles and overcome them.

Keep in touch with your goals and the benefits of mindfulness to these goals

Never lose touch on what you want to achieve as well as how mindfulness can help you reach your goals. Always think and ponder on these goals because once you bear them in mind, they will always motivate you to achieve your goals through practice and trainings, especially in times where distractions are everywhere.

Seek assistance

As beginners, it is not easy to start practicing mindfulness. So, as a tip, it helps when you seek assistance from experts. This way, you'll be guided in the right direction.

Practice mindfulness with someone

This refers to getting a partner who can practice mindfulness with you. You can try to practice mindfulness with your siblings, best friend, parents, colleagues, etc. The best thing about practicing with someone is that you don't have to go through the whole process yourself. They can lift you up you when you feel discouraged so you won't give up easily.

Conclusion

Happiness and contentment are basic goals of a person; a life that's free from worries. However, stressors and worry-triggers cannot be avoided leading people to give up on life or view their life as worthless. Living in the present, however, can help you live for today.

Remember, even if you worry about tomorrow, you will never know what will actually happen. Live your life one day at a time. This is possible if you practice mindfulness. Mindfulness not only gives you peace of mind and relieves stress; it also keeps you out of trouble. So, follow the mindfulness tips and techniques by heart, achieve mindfulness and learn to appreciate life at present.

Being in control of a mind, even for a brief period in the grand scheme of things, can help you diffuse tension - often for the other party, as well as yourself. It can also help you come across as more confident, outgoing and as someone who's interested in many things, and in other people.

So assess, fine-tune, improve and move toward mastery of controlling minds. It can enhance virtually every area of your life It can give you better physical health, mental clarity, emotional stability, spiritual peace, and even increased financial gain. It all depends on the situation, the conversation, and how you maneuver it to achieve your goals.

You're in the driver's seat - so talk with confidence, consideration and the continued willingness to improve this skill - and you'll wind up on the road to success - every time!